For my dear sister Yvonne and brother-in-law Duncan,
with love,
Jackie.

10 9 8 7 6 5 4 3 2 1
First published in the United Kingdom in 2000
by David Bennett Books Limited, United Kingdom.

Distributed by Sterling Publishing Company, Inc. 387, Park Avenue South, New York, N.Y. 10016.
Distributed in Canada by Sterling Publishing, c/o Canadian Manda Group,
One Atlantic Avenue, Suite 105, Toronto, Ontario, Canada M6K 3E7.

ISBN 0-8069-7539-3
Printed in China.

Farm Babies

Jacqueline
McQuade

Duckling

A baby duck is called a duckling.
*This duckling loves water, and puddles
are just as much fun as ponds!*

Lamb

A baby sheep is called a lamb.
*This woolly lamb just loves skipping through the meadow
in the warm spring sunshine.*

Kitten

A baby cat is called a kitten.
After playing outside, this little kitten has found
a cozy place in the barn for a rest.

Piglets

A baby pig is called a piglet.
*These pink little piglets have found a shady place
to lie down in the long, cool grass.*

Chicks

A baby chicken is called a chick.
*These chirpy little chicks love to nuzzle
into their mommy's soft feathers.*

Puppy

A baby dog is called a puppy.
*When he grows up, this little puppy will help around
the farm. Just now though, he spends his time exploring.*

Calf

A baby cow is called a calf.
Learning to walk on four wobbly legs is hard work,
so sometimes this little calf needs to take a rest.

Foal

A baby horse is called a foal.
This gentle little foal follows his mommy all the way
around the paddock on the soft grass.

The story of the

A Very Special Friend

Sally Ann Wright and Frank Endersby

Everywhere Jesus goes, people want to be near him.

Children come running to hear him tell stories on the mountainside.

'God loves you,' says Jesus. 'God cares about you more than anyone else.'

Everywhere Jesus goes, special things happen.

A man jumps up from his mat and carries it home. 'Look! Now I can walk!' he says.

A blind man throws away his stick and begging bowl. 'Look! Now I can see!' he shouts.

Everywhere Jesus goes, people know someone he has helped. So when Jesus rides a donkey into Jerusalem, they are pleased to see him. They shout and wave and cheer.

'Look! Here comes Jesus!'
'Hooray for Jesus our king!'

5

But there are some people who don't love Jesus. They frown and shake their heads.

'Why do people love Jesus?'

'Why don't they listen to us any more?'

'Let's find someone to betray him.'

Now it is time for Jesus and his friends to have supper. But what is Jesus doing?

Jesus is washing their feet. Jesus is drying them with a towel. Jesus is doing the servant's job!

'I am showing you how to love and take care of each other,' said Jesus. 'Always put others first and people will know you are my friends.'

This is the last time we will eat together,' says Jesus. 'Soon one of you will betray me to my enemies. One of you doesn't want to be my friend any more.

'Eat this bread – it is my body, broken for you. Drink this wine – it is my blood, shed for you.'

While they are eating, Judas, one of the twelve friends, goes out into the night.

Judas goes to the men who do not like Jesus. 'What will you give me if I betray Jesus to you?' he asks.

Judas leaves with thirty silver coins.

Jesus is praying among the olive trees, while his friends are watching, waiting, falling asleep.

'Help me, Father God,' he prays. 'Help me to be brave. Help me to do what you want me to do.'

Jesus hears the men coming through the olive trees. Jesus sees the lights from their torches.

Jesus sees his friend, Judas, who doesn't want to be his friend any more.

And unfriendly men march Jesus away while his friends are so frightened, they run away and hide.

11

Everywhere Jesus goes, his friends follow him
because they love him.

Where are his friends now?

Through the night people ask many questions, trying to trick Jesus. The Roman governor knows Jesus has done nothing wrong but he is afraid.

'Take him away,' he says to his soldiers.

On Friday morning, soldiers march Jesus away, through the gate, out of the town and up the hill, to die on a cross.

Everywhere Jesus goes, people want to be near him. Everywhere Jesus goes, special things happen. Everywhere Jesus goes, people know someone he has helped.

But today there is no one there to help him.

Some of Jesus' friends are watching and weeping.

'Take care of my mother,' Jesus says to his friend John.

'John can be your son now,' Jesus says to Mary, his mother.

Then Jesus takes his last breath and dies on the cross.

15

On Friday evening, one of Jesus' friends takes
down his body from the cross, wraps his
body in linen and puts him gently in a tomb in
a garden.

Weeping women follow to see where
Jesus lies behind a huge stone door, rolled
across a cave.

16

It is on Sunday morning, even before the sun is up, that Jesus' friend Mary and other women go to the garden with herbs and spices.

But someone has moved the heavy stone door! Angels are there in the garden!

'Jesus is not here,' they say. 'Jesus is alive!'

Mary doesn't understand. She knows that Jesus died. She saw his dead body buried. Mary stands weeping in the garden quite alone as the sun rises.

But Mary is not alone.

'Mary!' says a kind voice behind her, the kind voice of... 'Jesus! Master! You're alive!' she says through her tears.

Later that day, Jesus comes to see his friends.

The doors are locked. His friends are hiding because they are still afraid. But Jesus does not knock on the door. His friends do not let him in. Suddenly he is there – standing among them, talking to them!

Jesus is alive!

Thomas was not with the others when they saw Jesus.

'It can't be true,' he says. 'He died. I need to see him with my own eyes before I can believe it.'

A week later, Jesus comes again.

'Hello, Thomas,' Jesus says. 'Come and see the wounds for yourself.'

But Thomas doesn't need to any more. Here is Jesus! He is alive!

21

Another day, Jesus finds his friends fishing on Lake Galilee.

'Throw your net on the other side,' he calls to them. 'Then come and have breakfast with me!'

Everywhere Jesus goes, people want to be near him. Everywhere Jesus goes, special things happen. Now Jesus tells them about the Holy Spirit who will soon come to help them and be with them always so they do not need to be afraid again.

'Tell everyone what you have seen and heard,' says Jesus. 'Make sure everyone knows how much God loves them. That's why I have come to live among you. Tell everyone God wants them to be his friends.'

First edition 2020

Copyright © 2020 Anno Domini Publishing
www.ad-publishing.com
Text copyright © 2020 Sally Ann Wright
Illustrations copyright © 2020 Frank Endersby

Publishing Director: Annette Reynolds
Art Director: Gerald Rogers
Pre-production Manager: Doug Hewitt

Published 2020 by Authentic Media Ltd,
PO Box 6326, Bletchley, Milton Leynes, MKI 9GG
Conforms to EN7I and AS/NZS ISO 8124.

Printed and bound in China